SHARING EDEN

Green teachings from Jews, Christians and Muslims

D0034269

By **Natan Levy**, **David Shreeve**
and **Harfiyah Haleem**

Edited by **Lindsay Swan**

Kube Publishing in association with **The Conservation Foundation**

KUBE

the
CONSERVATION
foundation

First published in England by Kube Publishing Ltd
and The Conservation Foundation.

Kube Publishing Ltd
Markfield Conference Centre
Ratby Lane, Markfield
Leicestershire LE67 9SY

Tel: +44 (0) 1530 249230   Fax: +44 (0) 1530 249656

Website: www.kubepublishing.com
Email: info@kubepublishing.com

The Conservation Foundation
1 Kensington Gore
London
SW7 2AR

Tel: +44 (0) 20 7591 3111   Fax: +44 (0) 20 7591 3110

Website: www.conservationfoundation.co.uk
Email: info@conservationfoundation.co.uk

Design and layout by Linton Design (lintondesign.com)

Distributed by Kube Publishing Ltd

Copyright © 2012 The Conservation Foundation   0 '22

Sharing Eden is a Conservation Foundation Faith Works project.

The right of David Shreeve, Natan Levy and Harfiyah Haleem to be
identified as the Authors of this work is hereby asserted by them in
accordance with the Copyright, Design and Patents Act 1988.

ISBN: 978-1-84774-041-0 *paperback*

A CIP data record for this book is available from the British Library.

Printed by Imak Ofset   Istanbul - TURKEY

The authors

Natan Levy is the Rabbi of Shenley United Jewish Community. He is the Rabbinical Expert for the London School of Jewish Studies' Responsibility Unit and in 2009 was appointed as the Environmental Liaison to the Chief Rabbi's Office. From 2005 to 2008 he served as the Jewish Campus Chaplain for the Southwest of England. Born and educated in America, he is passionately concerned with issues of environmental justice and global morality.

David Shreeve is the Director of The Conservation Foundation which he co-founded in 1982. He is also the Environmental Adviser to the Archbishops' Council of the Church of England and co-author of *How Many Lightbulbs Does it Take to Change a Christian?* and *Don't Stop at the Lights*. He was awarded a Lambeth Degree in 2003 in recognition of his influence in helping the Church's understanding of environmental issues.

Harfiyah Haleem is the editor of a collection of essays on Islam and the Environment, co-editor of *The Muslim Green Guide to Reducing Climate Change* and treasurer to the trustees of the Islamic Foundation for Ecology and Environmental Sciences (IFEES). She works with people of all ages, giving talks and workshops to schools, universities and young people's groups, contributing to sustainability projects and is currently working on *How Green is Your Deen?*, an Islam TV Channel series for teenagers.

Edited by **Lindsay Swan**

Acknowledgements

The authors would like to thank these organisations for their help in preparing Sharing Eden:

The Conservation Foundation

The Board of Deputies of British Jews

IFEES – The Islamic Foundation For Ecology And Environmental Sciences

The Mercers Company and the Garfield Weston Foundation

In particular the authors would like to express gratitude to the following people:

David Shreeve thanks Rt Revd and Rt Hon Dr Richard Chartres, Bishop of London; Revd Rob Gillion and Revd Graham Rainford of Holy Trinity Sloane Square; Canon John Kiddle, Director of Mission, The Diocese of St Albans and Nick Reeves OBE, Executive Director of CIWEM.

Natan Levy would like to thank his fellow co-authors, Harfiyah and David; the Chief Rabbi Lord Jonathan Sacks; his wife, Ariella and his four children, Chava Temima, Saadya, Emuna, and Ezra – the trees we plant now, may you be blessed to eat of their future fruits.

Harfiyah Haleem gives her thanks to Rianne Ten Veen, to all the other people who helped produce this book and, finally, thanks to the One God we all worship, for making it possible.

The Jewish Texts are translated by Rabbi Natan Levy, with reference to the Jewish Publication Society Bible and the Adin Steinsaltz Talmud.

Contents

Introduction

Why?

Whatever their differences now and over the centuries, Christians, Jews and Muslims are the children of Abraham and still share many traditions in their teachings, worship and lifestyles. These shared traditions lie behind the decision to write this book about the three Abrahamic faiths' relationship with the environment, rather than all faiths. That may come later.

Sharing Eden can only begin to describe what would take many volumes if we were to go into all the details and issues, but we hope it will supply some of the answers which many from the three faiths, other faiths and indeed those of no faith, seek.

The Abrahamic faiths are complex creations of sub-divisions and sub-species evolved as a result of beliefs, politics, intuition, creativity, coincidence, revelation, inspiration, miracles and no doubt many other factors.

Simple things, hardly noticed and taken for granted, will have their reasons and meanings. For example, architectural features in places of worship, or the worship itself, will have a tradition that can be explained.

So look on this book as a 'start'. There is so much misinformation and misunderstanding in our world today that we can honestly say that we believe our task is simply to inform and *begin* to explain. We have absolutely no hidden agenda; there is no attempt to gain points or converts.

When it comes to the environment, we all have a role to play, whether or not we hold a faith. We hope this book shows that, as far as the followers of the Abrahamic faiths are concerned, they have no excuse not just to be aware, but also to be actively concerned, about the state of our world's environment.

Natan Levy, David Shreeve, Harfiyah Haleem

The three faiths' perspectives

A Jewish Environmental Ethic, Natan Levy

Life does not begin in the Garden of Eden. In Genesis you'll see a twist to the familiar story:

These are the products of the heaven and the earth when they were created on the day that the Lord God made earth and heaven – now all the trees of the field were not yet on the earth and all the herb of the field had not yet sprouted.

God formed the human, dirt from the ground, and breathed into him the breath of life. God planted a garden in Eden in the East, and placed the human that He had created within it. Genesis 2:4-8

God first creates a human (Adam) and later places him into the Garden. Why not just create Adam in the Garden itself? And, if not in the Garden, just *where* does Adam take his first breath? Genesis tells us that the setting into which Adam is born is no manicured garden, but a desert landscape. Adam wakes to a wasteland.

The 11th century Biblical commentator, Rashi, offers this insight into Adam's peculiar birthplace:

Even though the trees and grasses had been created on the third day of creation, until the creation of Man on day sixth, everything waited at the lip of the ground to sprout forth. And why did the flora wait? Because until the

appearance of Adam there was no one to realise how badly the grass needed
rain to grow, and no one to work and pray for change.   Genesis 2:5

The grass could have grown, the bushes could have burst forth,
but God wanted to teach humanity its first fundamental lesson:
when it comes to the environment, it is up to you to notice what
is lacking, and it is up to you to be the agents of change. Prayer
and work are the tools at your disposal. Do not let the world
remain barren, do not accept brokenness. That is the message
that God wished to impress upon Adam, and through him to all of
humanity. And as Adam was created to look upon a barren world
and feel its need for rain, we must listen to the needs of our own
fragile world. As the Jewish sages impart:

It is not up to you to finish the task, yet you are never free to desist from the
work.   Ethics of Our Fathers (Pirke Avot) 2:21

Entering the Garden of Eden, Adam is confronted with the task of
sustainability. A *Midrash*, a biblical allegory, relates that God said
to Adam:

Behold My works, how beautiful and commendable they are! All that I have
created, for your sake I created it. Pay heed that you do not corrupt and
destroy My universe, for if you corrupt it there is no one to repair it after
you.   Midrash Kohelet Rabbah 7:20

A Christian View of the Environment, David Shreeve

Since early times most Christians have used a public statement, The Apostles' Creed, (first formulated in Nicaea in AD 325), to confess their faith in Jesus Christ. It begins:

I believe in God, the Father Almighty, Maker of heaven and earth.

To most Christians the many divisions amongst their faith are not simply confusing - they are a mystery. So many denominations, sects, traditions, callings, customs, leaders... For those outside the faith it must all seem a conundrum that a man living a simple life two thousand years ago would be remembered and worshipped in so many complicated and often extreme ways.

Even the Lord's Prayer, the main prayer of Christian worship, taught by Jesus to his disciples, comes in various forms, but whichever version is used, its environmental message is fundamental and clear.

Our Father which art in heaven, Hallowed be thy name.
Thy Kingdom come. Thy will be done in earth, as it is in heaven.

Matthew 6:9-10

Some bibles do not include what is known as the Benedicite, the Song of Creation. In some it appears in the Book of Daniel, but it has been part of the Book of Common Prayer, first published in 1549, and is used in Anglican morning prayers and in Lauds in the Roman Catholic Office. The canticle covers much of creation of which the following is just a part:

O let the Earth bless the Lord: yea, let it praise him, and magnify him for ever.
O ye Mountains and Hills, bless ye the Lord: praise him, and magnify him for ever.
O all ye Green Things upon the Earth, bless ye the Lord: praise him, and magnify him for ever.

Christians have a particular responsibility to the environment because of the acknowledgement and worship of God as creator, redeemer and sustainer. Abuse of the natural world is disobedience to God, not merely an error of judgment.

Christians believe that planet earth belongs to God and that he entrusted it to humankind, made in his image and responsible to him. We are in the position of stewards, tenants, curators, trustees and guardians, whether or not we acknowledge this responsibility. It is easy to forget that the Earth is the Lord's and we must include humankind as just part of the living world that we share with all his creatures.

And God saw everything that he had made, and, behold, it was very good.

Genesis 1:31

In the New Testament, Jesus Christ is represented as at one with the Creator, sustainer and redeemer of the natural order as well as of humankind. As the Old Testament stories tell of order coming from chaos, so Christ brings order and meaning to a world damaged by human greed and misuse, emphasising God's care and concern for his creation. Christians, therefore, believe they have an obligation to offer worship and thanks for:

Creation, preservation and all the blessings of this life.

General Thanksgiving from the Prayer Book

It seems strange, therefore, that as Christian churches celebrate the fundamental events of the revelation of God in Christ, there has been no day and time in the liturgical calendar when Christians specifically remembered God as Creator. A start was made to rectify this in 1989 when the then Ecumenical Patriarch of Constantinople, Dimitrios 1, suggested to all Churches that they observe 1 September, the Orthodox Church's first day of its ecclesiastical year, as a day 'of the protection of the natural environment'. On this day they would offer 'prayers and supplications to the Maker of all, both in thanksgiving for the great gift of creation and in petition for its protection and salvation.'

Ten years later, the European Christian Environmental Network widened this proposal, urging churches to adopt a 'Time for Creation' stretching from 1 September to the second Sunday in October, a time especially extended to enable it to include the Feast Day of St Francis, patron saint of animals and ecology.

Be praised, my Lord God
in and through all your creatures
especially among them,
through noble Brother Sun
by whom you light the day
in his radiant splendid beauty
he reminds us, Lord, of you.

Be praised, my Lord God, through Sister Moon and all the stars,
You have made the sky shine in their lovely light.

In Brother Wind be praised, my Lord,
and in the air, in clouds and calm,
in all the weather moods that cherish life.

Laudes Creaturarum, St Francis of Assisi

Christ's demands go beyond the simple claims of justice, they require that any sacrifices be distributed according to capacity. This means that the main burdens of responsible action to help and protect our planet will fall on those in the more highly developed countries whatever their historical or present role in causing environmental degradation.

An Islamic Perspective, **Harfiyah Haleem**
(**Based on the Muslim Declaration on Nature, Assisi 1976**)

We are not masters of this Earth; it does not belong to us to do what we wish.
It belongs to God and He has entrusted us with its safekeeping.

The essence of Islamic teaching is that the entire universe
is God's creation. Allah makes the waters flow upon the
earth, upholds the heavens, makes the rain fall and keeps the
boundaries between day and night. The whole of the rich and
wonderful universe belongs to God, its maker, submits to Him and
glorifies Him. It is God who created the plants and the animals
in their pairs and gave them the means to multiply. Then God
created mankind - a very special creation because mankind alone
was created with reason and the power to think and even the
means to turn against his Creator. Mankind has the potential to
acquire a status higher than that of the angels or sink lower than
the lowliest of the beasts.

The word 'Islām' has the dual meaning of submission and peace.
Mankind is a specially honoured creation of Allah. But still
we are God's creation and we can only properly understand
ourselves when we recognise that our proper condition is one of
submission to the God who made us. We are not masters of this
Earth; it does not belong to us to do what we wish. It belongs to
God and He has entrusted us with its safekeeping. We bear the
burden of responsibility for the way in which we use or abuse the
trust of God (*amānah*).

The central concept of Islam is *tawhīd* or the Unity of God. Allah
is One: and His Unity is also reflected in the unity of mankind,
all sprung from the same soul, and the unity of man and nature,

all creatures of God. His human trustees are responsible for upholding the unity and balance (*mīzān*) of His creation, the integrity of the Earth, its flora and fauna, its wildlife and natural environment. We court disaster in this life (*dunya*) and the next (*ākhirah*) if we corrupt the balance and harmony of God's creation around us ('the environment').

So unity, trusteeship, balance and accountability (*tawhīd, amānah, mīzān* and *ākhirah*), are the pillars of the environmental ethics of Islam. They constitute the basic values taught by the Qur'ān and the Prophet Muhammad and translated into practical injunctions in the *Sharī'ah*.

The Lambeth Declaration

The Archbishop of Canterbury hosted a meeting of faith leaders and faith-based and community organisations at Lambeth Palace on 29 October 2009 to discuss the response of faith communities to environmental issues. As a result the meeting agreed The Lambeth Declaration.

Faith communities have a crucial role to play in pressing for changes in behaviour at every level of society and in every economic sector. We all have a responsibility to learn how to live and develop sustainably in a world of finite resources. Building on the examples of local and international action to live and to work together *The Lambeth Declaration* calls on the faith community to:

* build on the examples of local and international action to live and to work together sustainably;

* share best practice and redouble our efforts to reduce emissions that result from our institutional and individual activities;

* work with our partners, our sister churches and communities internationally to mitigate the effects of climate change on the poorest and most vulnerable communities in the developing world;

* press governments to support that effort.

To help to achieve these ends we agree to use today's meeting as the first step in an ongoing process of collaboration. We believe our communities can be key agents of change and urge the Government wherever possible to support our efforts to build capacity and commitment to reduce carbon emissions, raise awareness and promote sustainable practice.

Chapter 1
Sustainability and Waste

Sustainability has become one of today's most overused words as the people of the world recognise – at last – that the planet's natural resources are finite. We see too that many people have lifestyles which far exceed their real needs and are quite out of proportion to those of others. For our children's sake and the sakes of our children's children, we must look at how we live *now*, and consider the demands we make on the planet we share.

Because what we do and where we live differs from person to person, household to household, there can be few hard and fast rules. Living our lives in a sustainable way needs everyone to draw up their own basic rules and whilst many of these can be based on good old common sense, faiths will often provide guidelines for sustainable living which have been there through the ages and which include wasting less and buying only what we need. We must know our limits and live within them.

Why has it taken us so long to realise this? The writings of the Abrahamic faiths show that Jews, Christians and Muslims have always been taught to think about sustainability and waste as a matter of belief and survival. The texts that guided our forefathers are as relevant today as they were when they were written – maybe more so!

Jewish

We are guests here and must leave things as we found them. If there is one idea the monotheistic faiths might teach the world it would be this:

The Earth and its fullness are the Lord's   Psalm 24:1

Even though we may live in a place of plenty, we have a duty to care for what we have, making sure to replace what we use for future generations. This is the essence of living sustainably:

When you come into the land, you will plant   Leviticus 19:23

A famous parable in the Talmud teaches this very lesson:

One day Honi was journeying on the road and he saw a man planting a carob tree. He asked, 'How long does it take for this tree to bear fruit?' The man replied, 'Seventy years.' Honi then further asked him. 'Are you certain that you will live another seventy years?' The man replied, 'Just as I found a world full of carob trees planted by my parents and grandparents, so I will plant for my children.'   Talmud Ta'anit 23a

It is easier to understand the moral responsibility to act in a particular way if we believe there is someone to whom we owe responsibility; that we are not owners of the planet but linked by covenant to those who come after us. Like the planter of the carob tree in the parable, we act so that those who come after us will have a world to enjoy as we did.

The simplest image, and surely the most sensible one, in thinking about our ecological responsibilities is to see the earth as belonging to the source of being, and us as its trustees, charged with conserving and if possible

beautifying it for the sake of our grandchildren not yet born.

Chief Rabbi Jonathan Sacks, 'The Dignity of Difference'

The injunction not to waste, the law of Bal Taschit, is one of the fundamental commands in the Torah. It comes from Deuteronomy 20:19-20, where Israel is told that even in a time of war, fruit bearing trees must not be cut down to build siegeworks – the vision of a sustainable world must never be abandoned:

When you besiege a city for many days to wage war against it to seize it, do not destroy the trees by swinging an axe against them, for from it you will eat, and you shall not cut it down; is the tree of the field a man that it too shall be besieged?

Deuteronomy 20:19

Later the Sages of Israel expanded the law to include any kind of wasteful activity.

Jews believe that we must utilise the world's natural bounty with consciousness and foresight. Nearly 5,000 acres of the Amazon rainforest will be cut down in the time it will take you to read this small book. Almost a quarter of the food found in our rubbish bins is perfectly usable, unopened and within its sell-by date.

Regard all living things as God's property. Destroy none, abuse none, waste nothing, employ all things wisely... look upon all creatures as servants in the household of creation.

Rabbi Samson Raphael Hirsch

21

Christian

The issue of sustainable development is consistent with Christian beliefs concerning creation and humanity's stewardship of it all.

For many people modern life has become a status of plenty, but is not sustainable because it involves so much waste. Products are soon discarded adding to already hugely wasteful packaging and the need for replacement.

Not much is known about Jesus's own lifestyle, but it would appear that he lived simply and wished others to do likewise:

Foxes have holes and birds of the air have their nests; but the Son of man hath not where to lay his head.   Matthew 8:20; Luke 9:58

Christian worship often quotes the Old Testament message:

Love thy neighbour as thyself.   Leviticus 19:18.

When Jesus was asked by young man who had kept all the Ten Commandments what did he still lack, Jesus answered:

If thou wilt be perfect, go and sell that thou hast, and give to the poor, and thou shalt have treasure in heaven: and come and follow me.   Matthew 19:21

Today it is the poor who are the first casualties of any changing climate.

And what do we do with waste? If everywhere is in the sight of God, there can be nowhere called 'away' where we can throw things.

Jesus was crucified outside the walls of Jerusalem on a site also used for dumping rubbish. Today we not only produce more rubbish than we can cope with, but much of it causes

 further problems of pollution by poisoning the earth, the water and life. This is not just happening in our own environments, but the rich countries are also dumping waste on poor countries and contaminating other lands rather than treating the problem where it occurs.

The Ecumenical Patriarch of Constantinople has been dubbed 'The Green Pope' after declaring pollution a sin. Actually the Patriarch went much further by saying:

To commit a crime against the natural world is a sin. For human beings to cause species to become extinct and to destroy the biological diversity of God's creation; for human beings to degrade the integrity of the earth by causing changes in its climate, by stripping the earth of its natural forests, or by destroying its wetlands; for human beings to injure other human beings with disease by contaminating the earth's waters, its land, its air, and its life, with poisonous substances – all of these are sins.

His All Holiness the Ecumenical Patriarch Bartholomew I

Since 1995, the Patriarch has been bringing together leaders of religion, science and the environment on floating symposia which have sailed to various world sites of environmental concern. The first was held as part of the celebration of the 1900th anniversary of the composition by St John the Theologian of the Book of Revelation and ended on Patmos with a service close to the hillside cave, where, according to legend, John compiled the Book of Revelation.

Muslim

Do not be wasteful: God does not like wasteful people.

Qur'an 6:141

The Qur'an and the example of the Prophet teach Muslims to live simply and not waste resources. The ecological footprint of most Muslim countries is still far smaller than those of Western and other developed countries.

In traditional Muslim economies, little is wasted. In Egypt, the stems and leaves of maize are fed to cattle, the ears to poultry and the dried cobs used as fuel for cooking. Cattle dung is used to fertilise the fields.

It is only in modern, centralised, mass-production economies that so much waste has been created – butter mountains, wine lakes, festering and poisonous landfill sites for rubbish, industrial pollution and so on.

Modern Muslim countries are not exempt from this, and some have even been 'persuaded' to take hazardous chemical waste from Western countries. Plastic bags litter their streets and deserts, killing many animals that eat them.

Some Muslims living in Western countries can still remember the old frugal ways, but it takes a big effort to counteract the flood of packaging, excess food and industrial consumer goods that people are encouraged to buy now.

The servants of the Lord of Mercy are those who walk humbly on the earth, ...those who are neither wasteful nor niggardly when they spend, but keep to a just balance.
                                                                    Qur'an 25:63–7

Do not squander your wealth wastefully: those who squander are brothers of Satan, and Satan is most ungrateful to his Lord.   Qur'an 17:26–27

"I heard the Prophet (pbuh) say: 'Every ummah (nation) has a test to undergo'. My ummah will be tried through wealth."   Hadith: Tirmidhi

Examples, actions and ideas

- Recycling is one way in which we can save our streets and countryside from disappearing under piles of rubbish. Churches have been involved in recycling for years providing their communities with opportunities to collect and recycle clothing and other goods at jumble sales. This is no trendy fad, but a practical and sensible way of extending the life and usage of our belongings. From mobile phones to ink cartridges, almost everything can be recycled, (www.recyclenow.com) Garden tools too can have a new lease of life through The Conservation Foundation's Tools Shed programme, which gives tools repaired by prisoners to schools and community gardens, (www.conservationfoundation.co.uk).

- Reduce consumption by not buying more than you need, avoiding packaged goods, and using everything up. The Torah law of Bal Taschit reminds us to eat within our limits. Sharing wealth is central to Islamic practice, especially through the welfare due, Zakat, which is the third pillar of Islam. In Christian churches Bring and Buy sales also enable those with creative skills to produce things for others in the community.

- Give surplus goods away to charities and exchange them in such schemes as Freecycle, (www.uk.freecycle.org) to help avoid waste by ensuring that things are reused. A new home can be found for almost everything, be it redundant spectacles or outmoded computers.

- London's Muslim communities have various projects to promote sustainable living and recycling. Practical advice is included in sermons (khutbahs) in mosques, on the stalls outside afterwards and in women's workshops. Children's activities include re-use and recycling such as making things with what is there – for example plastic bottles – teaching useful sustainability lessons along the way. Demonstrations and information are available at events and 'Green Jihad' has been declared on trash in a campaign organised by IFEES (Islamic Foundation For Ecology and Environmental Sciences) which includes a short, humorous and controversial film 'Clean Medina', where young British Muslims in Birmingham have joined together in a 'people action' to make their city greener, (www.ifees.org.uk).

❄ In Chile, a community self-help project run by a small Anglican NGO called Corporacion Anglicana de Misión y Desarrollo (CAMDES) provides work, skills and income so reducing the number of men and young people who leave their families and communities to find work in the cities.

❄ Planting more than just carob trees, small eco-gardens are sprouting up in urban landscapes throughout the UK. One such is Gan Teva, the London School of Jewish Studies organic garden project, where Jewish wisdom teaches hands-on sustainable gardening for children and adults, focused on core Jewish values, (www.lsjs.ac.uk).

❄ A Jewish community-based organisation in the United States is committed to rescuing leftover food from restaurants and catered events to feed the hungry. Every day 'Table to Table' sends out its four refrigerated trucks to various locations in New York and New Jersey to collect fresh food that would have otherwise ended up in landfill and redistributes to Homeless shelters, HIV clinics, battered women shelters and many more locations, (www.tabletotable.org). In the UK, GIFT, a Jewish charity, does the same, encouraging and promoting giving and volunteering in the community, (www.jgift.org).

❄ The UK charity FareShare redistributes surplus food to disadvantaged people in the community and at the same time minimises the food sent to landfill (www.fareshare.org.uk).

Chapter 2
Water

Water is at the heart of the rituals of the Abrahamic faiths, symbolising spiritual purity and new beginnings. Its place in worship is fundamental. It is a vital element for a clean and healthy life, as well as the stuff of survival, for without water we cannot survive. It has often been scarce, which is when it is most highly valued. Under control it can not only mean good health and well-being, but also safety and power. Out of control it can bring death and destruction. There have always been droughts and storms. Religious stories feature water as the source of food, the provider of sustenance, the saviour of a people, the cleanser of souls. When there is sufficient, so much is often wasted and yet there is less clean water now than there has ever been. Water is life: we need to share it fairly and we abuse it at our peril.

Jewish

Water is so vital to human survival, that the prophet Jeremiah referred to God as the *Source of Living Waters.*   *Jeremiah* 2:12

And the Jewish sages simply say *Water is life.*

Avot of Rabbi Natan 34:10.

Why was Moses chosen as leader of Israel? Perhaps because at a lonely well in the desert of Midian, a group of shepherds had monopolised the water, pushing out the weaker newcomers. Moses stood up against this injustice and intervened for a fair share of this most precious resource for all.

The minister of Midian had seven daughters; they came and drew water and filled the troughs to water their father's sheep. The shepherds came and drove them away. Moses got up and saved them and watered their sheep.

Exodus 2:17

884 million people lack access to safe drinking water. Who amongst us will stand up like Moses, for the rights of these?

Water is cheap and wine is expensive (and yet) it is possible for the world to live without wine; it is impossible for the world to live without water.

Talmud Yerushalmi, Horayot, Chapter 3, halacha 5

If we were to walk in the woods and a spring appeared just when we became thirsty, we would call it a miracle. And if on a second walk, we became thirsty at just that point again, and again the spring appeared, we would remark on the coincidence. But if that spring were there always, we would take it for granted and cease to notice it. Yet is that not more miraculous still?

The Ba'al Shem Tov.

The miracle of clean, potable water is a communal right, and no one is exempt from the obligation to provide water for public use.

Everyone in a community, even the orphans and the scholars that are normally exempted from community taxes, are required to pay their share of creating and maintaining water sources for the community.

Talmud Bavli, Baba Batra 8a

Christian

And God said, Let the waters under the heaven be gathered together unto one place, and let the dry land appear: and it was so. And God called the dry land Earth; and the gathering together of the waters called he Seas: and God saw that it was good. Genesis 1:9-10

Jesus was baptised by John the Baptist in the River Jordan.

And Jesus, when he was baptized, went up straightway out of the water: and lo, the heavens were opened unto him, and he saw the Spirit of God descending like a dove, and lighting upon him.
Matthew 3:16

Christians continue this link using water in services of baptism for all ages. For some, baptism still involves total immersion in rivers or the sea or in special

tanks within their churches. Young children are often welcomed into the Christian family at a Christening service which involves the priest sprinkling water from the font onto the child's head whilst promises are made by 'Godparents'. Traditionally the font is an octagon, a shape midway between a square symbolising earth and a circle symbolising God, which together combine to be a symbol of Jesus – unifying God and earth. Often inscribed with the monogram IHS, the font is situated close to the entrance to the building at the start of the central aisle which represents the Christian's journey through life towards God.

Water is also used for other Christian blessings and is thrown by the priest spraying those or things being blessed with a brush or branch known as an aspergill.

Christians recall Jesus washing the feet of his disciples during the Last Supper with priests washing the feet of their congregation, especially on Maundy Thursday.

During the Eucharist, or communion service, some Christians add water to the wine to remember how water as well as blood came out of Jesus's body when he died on the cross.

At the entrance of some, especially Roman Catholic, churches, there is a stoup of holy water. This descendant of the Jewish custom of ritual washing evolved from a fountain in early churches to a small recessed bowl close to the entrance to enable worshippers to be spiritually clean before entering the building.

Muslim

*Who created the heavens and earth? Who sends down
water from the sky for you? ... Is it another god beside
God? No!*   Qur'an 27:60

*He sends water down from the sky to restore the earth to life
after death.*   Qur'an 30:24

*If all your water were to sink into the earth, who then could
give you flowing water?*   Qur'an 67:30

In a desert land like Arabia, where the Prophet Muhammad (pbuh)
was born, water is always a scarce resource. According to a hadith
in al-Bukhari on the story of Hagar and Ismail, the discovery of
the Well of Zamzam in Mecca was the key factor in establishing
them and the descendants of Prophet Ibrahim there. In the
Qur'an, Ibrahim and Ismail are shown building the Ka'ba nearby
as the first house of worship for the One God in Mecca and
praying that their descendants would continue to worship Him.

Although washing and cleanliness are obligatory for Muslims
before the formal prayer, and so on, the Prophet (pbuh) used only
a few handfuls of water to do this and a small bowlful to clean
His whole body. When there is no water available, clean sand,
dust or stones can be used instead. The Prophet (pbuh) advised
moderation, even in drinking water with meals, so as to leave
enough space in one's stomach for 'easy breathing'.

Islamic law provides clear rules for sharing out water for irrigation among all those who live within reach of it, and in the 1,000 years of Islamic civilisation engineers built cisterns, aqueducts and underground canals (qanat) to supply fresh water to cities like Sana'a in Yemen and Cordoba in Muslim Andalusia.

Many Muslims still live in countries where water is in short supply. Where the supply is centralised, as in Abu Dhabi, measures are being taken to use clean waste (grey) water for irrigation, to save clean water for drinking.

God's Messenger appeared while Saad was making the ablutions. When he saw that Saad was using a lot of water, he intervened saying, 'What is this? You are wasting water.' Saad replied asking, 'Can there be wastefulness while making the ablutions?' To which God's Messenger replied, 'Yes, even if you make them on the bank of a rushing river.' Extravagance is to use water without any benefit, like washing the parts more than three times.

Hadith: Ibn Majah

Pouring some water out of your bucket into that of your brother counts as an act of charity. Hadith: Muslim and Tirmidhi

Examples, actions and ideas

❋ Water is something all households can save by using less and some can harvest rainwater in water butts for their own use and to share with others. We can do the same when watering our gardens and pot-plants and take special care not to run excess water from the taps or leave them running or dripping.

❋ The Church of South India is promoting green water initiatives by digging mud pits in all its church land and on the land of its congregations to harvest rainwater and recharge groundwater. Since June 2009 each member of the church has been asked to dig one pit to harvest rainwater from their rooftops.

❋ A few handfuls of water are sufficient for washing before Muslim prayers. East London and Palmers Green Mosques in London, for example, have special water-saving taps.

❋ The Muslim Khatri Association runs a community centre in Leicester. The centre has many environment-friendly features but the former shoe warehouse needed a complete makeover. Its water is conserved with waterless urinals and push taps with restricted flows.

Bio-filter for Kfar-Sava, Isra

✻ In the arid region of Israel there are some of the most innovative solutions for conserving and recycling water. Drip irrigation invented for Israel's harsh desert conditions now helps curtail water evaporation on farms around the world. Currently the Jewish National Fund is pioneering a new project to filter urban run-off using 'bio-filtering' – a mixture of soils and plants – that cleans the water of harmful chemicals. To find out about bio-filtering and other new water projects visit the Jewish National Fund at www.kkl.org.il and follow links to 'Water for Israel'.

Bio-filter construction at Kfar-Sava, north of Tel-Aviv

Chapter 3
Energy and Natural Resources

So much of the world depends on energy, mainly created from finite natural resources, for what have become the essentials of our daily life. Without it the complex communications and information systems on which we now rely, would be rendered useless. The quest for energy creates international tensions, uneasy alliances and ethical dilemmas and threatens the future of the planet.

There has never been so much energy available as there is today. Technology is turning sun, wind and tides into energy to add to what we currently call 'conventional sources'. In the West, we are committed to instant power. Some lives are totally dependent on it whilst for others elsewhere it remains a dream as they struggle to study with a single light from simple sources unchanged for generations.

But as the scriptures reveal, the challenge is not new: energy sources have always been precious.

Jewish

There are two ways we humans can gather energy. There is the energy we pull up from hell, as it were: oil, gas, coal, which have in common that they dump carbon into the atmosphere and are exhaustible. Then there is the energy we draw from heaven: tide, wind, and sun. When *we* speak of energy, let us learn to look towards heaven.

The energy contained in nature, in the earth and its waters, in the atom and the sunshine will not avail us if we fail to activate the most precious vital energy: the moral spiritual energy inherent in humankind, in the inner recesses of our being, in our mysterious, uncompromising, unfathomable, and divinely inspired soul.　　　　　　　David Ben Gurion

According to the ancient sages every person must say that the entire world was created for me. If the world was created for me, it follows that I must always examine how I can rectify the world and fulfil its needs and pray for its healing.
　　　　　　　Rabbi Nachman of Bratslav, Likkutai M'HaRan 1, 5:1

If one Jew sins, all of Israel feels it... This can be compared to the case of a man on a ship who began to drill a hole under his own seat. His fellow travellers asked him, 'What are you doing?' He replied, 'What concern is it to you: do you not see that I am only drilling under my own place?' 'Yet', they continued, 'when the water comes up it will drown us all!'　　Vayikra Rabbah 4:6

The man on the ship who bores a hole under his own seat, oblivious to the other passengers, is the critical parable of our age. Each day we continue to expel ever more carbon into the sky. In this frail ark we call 'earth' no one can ever say: 'I have the right to make a hole if I desire it!' We are devouring our limited resources at a ferocious rate, consuming energy with abandon. Will our children not turn to us one day and say: 'Did you fail to realise that when the water comes up it will drown us all?'

Archimedean Screw hydro-electric system on the River Dart

Christian

Praise be to the Holy Trinity! God is sound and life, Creator of the Universe, Source of all life, whom the angels sing; wondrous Light of all mysteries known or unknown to humankind, and life that lives in all.   Hildegard of Bingen

Much of the world has become totally committed to using energy without any regard to future supplies and its effect on our planet. Many of us have become world travellers – especially the young, who travel to celebrate the end of formal education and the older generation, who have the time and money and consider it their right to see the world after a lifetime of service. We have become dependent on our personal transport. Not for us a dark place to live and work – energy is the source for our light, heat and freedom.

The problem is that for many in our world this is not possible and they are paying the price with insufficient means.

In the United States, Interfaith Power and Light is working to help church congregations be models of energy efficiency, utilise renewable energy, and to lead by showing a strong example of stewardship of creation. The organisation actively campaigns to support public policies to reduce society-wide US emissions to a sustainable level, (www.interfaithpowerandlight.org).

The Church of England is endeavouring to set an example by putting its own house in order. Its environmental campaign, 'Shrinking the Footprint', seeks to enable the whole Church to address – in faith, practice and mission – the issues of environment and climate change. The first task is to review and monitor the energy use in all its churches and cathedrals, offices, clergy homes and schools.

A New Testament containing gospels written in very different times, in a very different environment to much of today's developed world, is unlikely to have scripture specifically about energy saving to draw upon, but 'loving our neighbours' must be to have concern for their well-being and not to cause them problems. Do we need so much light inside and outside our buildings? Do we need to heat the whole building, even when it is not in use? How do we get to and from it – is there a better way?

One of the major themes of the Christian faith is 'renewal'. We simply cannot use up all our resources to provide the energy for today's needs. In the Book of Revelation we find the message of the tree of life sustaining the nations and there is no more darkness. The water of life nourishes the tree and the tree nourishes the nations. We must consider today how the cycle is to continue with our ever increasing demands.

And he shewed me a pure river of water of life, clear as crystal, proceeding out of the throne of God and of the Lamb. In the midst of the street of it, and on either side of the river, was there the tree of life, which bare twelve manner of fruits, and yielded her fruit every month: and the leaves of the tree were for the healing of the nations.   Revelation 22:1-2

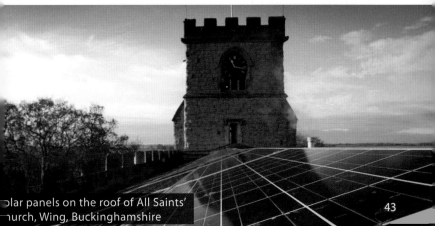

Solar panels on the roof of All Saints' Church, Wing, Buckinghamshire

43

Muslim

Consider the fire you kindle: is it you who make the wood for it grow or We? Qur'an 56:71-2

It is He who produces fire for you out of the green tree – lo and behold! – from this you kindle fire." Qur'an 36:80

Did we not build seven strong heavens above you and make [the sun] a blazing torch? Qur'an 78:12-13

We harnessed the stormy wind for Solomon. Qur'an 21:81

Aishah said: 'A complete month would pass by during which we would not make a fire (for cooking), and our food used to be only dates and water unless we were given a present of some meat.' Hadith: Muslim

The Prophet Muhammad (pbuh) hardly ever lit a fire to cook in his house. He lived on dates, milk and barley bread and only ate meat if someone gave him a piece.

Eating raw fruit and vegetables, especially those grown locally and in season

Eat of their fruit in their season
Qur'an 6:141

or cooking them only lightly, reduces the need to use energy in their production, transport and in the home. In Egypt, until very recently, most bread was baked using dried corn-cob fires inside clay ovens, and this flat bread cooks very quickly, requiring minimal fuel supplies. Energy needed to heat and cool buildings was also reduced by the use of insulating materials like thick mud or stone walls. Buildings were designed to allow cool air to circulate freely, such as those with cooling towers in early Iranian architecture or houses with open central courtyards. Much less noisy than air conditioners too!

Muslims were among the first to use ice for refrigeration. Saladin presented Richard the Lionheart with some peach sorbet when he was ill. They obtained the ice from mountains and kept it underground in special ice cellars. No energy was needed for this except to dig the cellars and fetch the ice (renewable human and animal energy).

In the Golden Age of Islamic Civilisation (9th-17th centuries CE) energy for mass production machinery (in mills) was produced by renewable means: wind, water, animals and human beings. Many Muslim countries such as Egypt and Morocco still use water power (hydro-electricity) to generate electricity for their modern economies. Some, Tunisia for example, now have wind farms and solar arrays to make use of the plentiful supply of sun. It is thought that a giant solar array in the Sahara Desert could power the whole of Europe.

Examples, actions and ideas

- The Church of South India promotes the use of community biogas plants using cow dung and human waste as cooking and for lighting in villages.

- An eco-mosque running on renewable energy opened in Levenshulme, Manchester in 2008. The Markaz al-Najmi Mosque has solar panels, under-floor heating and low energy bulbs, and is built with wood and Indian pink stone. It fuses Eastern and Western architecture, and is furnished with peach-coloured deep pile carpets and a chandelier.

- The Muslim Khatri Association community centre in Leicester uses a large solar photovoltaic system. Electricity is saved on low-energy lighting with intelligent controls and the walls have been insulated with sheep wool, which not only hugely decreases the heat loss/gain through the walls but also requires less energy to produce than standard mineral wool insulation products. Low-VOC (Volatile Organic Compound) paints were used for decoration, and natural marmoleum, made from linseed oil, was used as a floor covering. The roof was redesigned to be south-facing for the PV panels, which generate electricity from the sun. The system cost £60,000 but will save money on fuel bills in the long-term. The solar electric system is now the biggest in the Midlands. The centre estimates that CO_2 savings are around 1.5 tonnes a year, (www.mka.org.uk).

- The non-profit Desertec Foundation, (www.desertec.org) and the industrial initiative it helped to found, (www.dii-eumena.com), are working with North African countries on the rollout of solar and wind power to meet fast-growing local demand and to export to their European neighbours. The Desertec Foundation is also active in East Asia.

✻ There are simple ways we can use less energy. Consider spending one day a week without driving or consuming or even turning on your television. For Jews that day is embedded in their tradition, it's called the Sabbath – a day of rest for all God's creatures.

Interfaith send-off at Lambeth Palace for the Rabbi Relay Ride.

✻ In order to encourage the Jewish community to get on their bikes, 2012 was designated the Big Green Jewish Year of the Bicycle. One event, the Rabbi Relay Ride, started at Land's End and finished at John O'Groats (the final leg being ridden by Rabbi Natan Levy).

✻ Monitor the heating regularly and don't overheat the water. A one degree increase in temperature increases fuel use by 6-10%.

St Mark's Church in Dalston, London has the only working turret barometer in Europe

Chapter 4

Climate Change

Climate change is one of the greatest challenges of our times. With so many different and often conflicting views coming from scientists, politicians, campaigners and the media, it is hard to find a way through all the *noise.* Concerns about climate change are not new and so, if we feel there is nothing we can do or don't know where to look, sometimes a way forward can be found in the texts of Judaism, Christianity and Islam. Climates do change and always have. What cannot be denied is how climate knows no limits – it affects everything. Nature, land, property, livelihoods will need to cope with changes. Members of faiths belong to large, international families far greater than the major environmental organisations or political parties. Within those families are people living in very different circumstances and, even though they may never meet those who have the means, they can feel responsible and contribute to the welfare of others. Modern media show us instant news of disasters, many of which would have otherwise remained unknown – except to those suffering. Faiths, as international communities, can resolve to support, learn and adapt.

Jewish

The problem of climate change is just too big, so nothing I do will make a difference! I'll admit it, I've harboured such thoughts. Perhaps you have too – we're a small cog in a big wheel. Yet a central theme of Judaism is that small individual acts, carefully performed over a lifetime, are of divine significance, these acts are called 'mitzvot', roughly translated as commandments, but actually from the Hebrew root-word for binding and joining. For these mitzvot – which guide a committed Jewish life from waking to sleeping and all the moments in-between – link our lives with God: that is to say, they invest each small act with cosmic meaning.

A Jewish saying goes:

In one pocket every person should place a note: 'For myself alone was this world created.' When you fear that you alone are not enough to change the world, reach into this pocket. In the other pocket, write another note: 'I am but dust and ashes.' Reach into this pocket when you think that you alone can change the world.

The tale of Noah and the Flood provides a first lesson in our very human ability to wreak unparalleled havoc upon our fragile globe:

God saw that the wickedness of Humanity was great upon the earth, and that the inclinations of their hearts were only turned to evil. God regretted having created Humanity on the earth and He had heartfelt sadness. God said, 'I will blot out these humans I have created from the face of the earth and the animals beside – from creeping critters to the birds of the sky, for I regret having made them'.   Genesis 6:5-7

The Flood narrative is a climate message for our age. The natural world can be sustained or destroyed by the moral choices we make each day. We have been fashioned to become a *little less than God,* (Psalm 8) and our every decision has global ramifications. Modern thinkers have coined a term for an epoch in history where human choices effect global ecological change, they call it the 'Anthropocene Age'. From the very first moment, when Adam was created 'in the image of God' (Genesis 1:27), the Bible has prepared humanity to live wisely in this age where our actions have the potential to alter the face of the earth.

Maimonides expressed a similar notion in his 11th century treatise on repentance:

Throughout the year everyone should regard himself and the world as if evenly poised between innocence and guilt. If he commits a sin he tilts the balance of his life and that of the world to guilt, causing destruction. If he performs a good deed he shifts the balance of his fate and that of the world to innocence, bringing salvation and deliverance to others. That is the meaning of the biblical phrase 'the righteous person is the foundation of the world' (Proverbs 10:25), namely that by an act of righteousness we influence the fate of, and save, the entire world. Mishne Torah, Hilchot Tshuvah 3:4

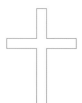

Christian

Climate change is seen as a political issue, an environmental issue and an economic issue. Christians believe that it is also a moral issue and share with other religions the belief that God has given humans a role as stewards of the Earth.

Whilst many matters have their natural place amongst the Christian calendar and liturgy, it is the fact that the role of humankind and the lifestyles of so many could be causing climate change that makes Christians question the consequences and theology of their beliefs and actions.

Religious buildings can often be the oldest buildings in the community witnessing the changes both people-made and natural throughout many generations. They will have seen communities come and go and many stand witness to wars, plagues, famines

St George's Church, Wroth

and pestilence. Damage from storms, politics, neglect and vandalism will have all been contained over the centuries of care and adaptation. Their structure may have been a result of chance or fashion, but often the design will have been proven many times to have withstood the ravages of time and could serve us well in years to come providing a place for the community to gather, shelter and remain dry or cool. Church records and memorials show how our forebears lived and adjusted to change.

Diverse as Christianity is, it is not surprising that views differ over the science and evidence of climate change. Whilst there are many for whom it the most urgent of the world's issues threatening humankind's very existence, others do not see it as something our actions can or should change. Scientists, like Christians, will always argue, but climate change has brought the environment to the forefront of today's challenges and this book is just one of many examples of how faiths are agreeing that stewardship of the planet is a fundamental concern. How we exploit it and manage its resources are concerns which Christians share increasingly both amongst themselves and with other faiths.

Few Christians can have lived without seeing change. One recent change will have been the observance of the Sabbath. Today we share a world where different days of the week are considered the Sabbath. Whether it is the human body or the land, everything needs its Sabbath to rest and reflect. It may be a day or just some moments during a day, the Sabbath is important and its observance can be vital in decreasing our demands on physical energy and mental well-being:

> *And God blessed the seventh day and sanctified it.*   Genesis 2:3

Muslim

Heat and cold, winds, clouds and rain are what make up the earth's climate, and they are changing all the time. There have been ice ages and tropical ages, even in the UK, but scientists now observe that the earth is warming inexorably, the polar ice-caps are melting faster and faster and that this is causing unusual climate events like hurricanes and tornadoes to multiply. Natural disasters, floods, storm surges, droughts etc. are much more common now than they were in the last century and large parts of low-lying countries, many of them inhabited by Muslims, like the Maldives and Bangladesh, may be inundated permanently within a few decades as sea levels rise. There are already hundreds of thousands of environmental refugees.

We bring down water from the sky for you to drink – you do not control its sources.
Qur'an 15:22

Are you sure that He who is in Heaven will not send a whirlwind to pelt you with stones?
Qur'an 67:16-17

Yet they will continue in their disbelief, even if We send a [scorching] wind and they see their crops turn yellow.
Qur'an 30:51

We let a roaring wind loose on them for a few disastrous days to make them taste the punishment of shame in this world. Qur'an 41:16

We have destroyed many a community that once revelled in its wanton wealth and easy living: since then their dwelling places have barely been inhabited – We are the only heir. Qur'an 28:58

There is wide scientific consensus that global warming is largely induced by the burning of fossil fuels for industrial and domestic purposes starting with the UK's industrial revolution in the 18th century CE. As the cause is human, so must be the solution. Unfortunately though, international agreements so far, like the Kyoto Protocol to limit fossil fuel emissions, have not been unanimous. New countries have started to emit more gases and big emitters have refused to reduce theirs. To turn our industrial systems around to cleaner, renewable fuels will take a massive effort from everyone, for the sake of those on earth after us and for the sake of our duty to God.

Examples, actions and ideas

❈ Change your power supply tariff to a green energy supplier.

❈ Invest in whatever renewable energy generation devices you can afford.

❈ Reduce use of cars and fossil-fuel heating.

❈ Use bicycles for short journeys and errands – like going to the place of worship: with a bike we can beat the parking problems, save money on fuel and get some healthy exercise.

❈ Christian churches, parishes, dioceses and groups are often linked to others elsewhere in the world where changes in climate may be more advanced or have greater consequences.

❈ The Church of England, in partnership with Tearfund, has established the Climate Justice Fund so that churches and congregations can contribute funds based on their carbon use to help practical action being undertaken by churches in other countries experiencing the effects of climate change, (www.climatejusticefund.org).

❈ One of the main priority areas of the burgeoning environmental movement in the Muslim world is the greening of the Hajj, the great pilgrimage to Mecca. The Green Hajj is both a revival of the exemplary ecological ethics of Islam and a rejection of the culture of conspicuous consumption and wastage. From a reduced consumption of plastic bags and bottles, to careful choices on transport, the aim is to reinstate the Hajj as a model of environmental behaviour. A first step was to build a high speed rail link between Jeddah, Mecca and

Mecca Metro

Madina, which was already in action during the Hajj in August-September 2010, reducing the need for cars and buses that emit carbon and heat.

❄ The Jewish Climate Change Campaign is inspired by the ancient Jewish calendar of a seven year sabbatical cycle. In 2015, when the next sabbatical year concludes, the campaign hopes to encourage at least 600,000 Jewish families (the same number who witnessed revelation at Mount Sinai) to create more sustainable and climate friendly lifestyles, (www.jewishclimatecampaign.org).

PUMKINS
AND SQUASH

BuHernut squash
(variety Ponca)

HOKIDO

Chapter 5
Food

What we eat, in what quantities and the rituals pertaining to food, is of great importance to the Abrahamic faiths. Food can be linked to specific times and seasons and whilst the meal is an opportunity to build and strengthen relationships, celebrate friendships and families and extend worship, it is also an opportunity to give thanks for its growth, harvest, production and supply. Meals are also occasions where thought can be spared for those without food, shelter and companionship.

Faiths teach the need to manage the natural resources and to guard against introducing unnatural products into food. Whilst some go hungry, others are wasteful. Food raises questions as to why and how this can happen and encourages us to think about the season for food, its production and transportation and whether we are really being fair.

Jewish

It is forbidden to enjoy anything in this world
without first uttering a blessing to God.

Talmud Berachot 35a

It is written, 'The earth and its fullness are God's', Psalms 24:1. Yet is it not
also written, 'He has given the earth to the children of man.' Psalms 115:16?
This is no contradiction. The first verse is before man's blessing, and the
second verse is after the blessing.

Talmud - Berachot 35a

To one for whom bread is suitable, give bread; to the one who needs dough,
give dough; to one for whom money is required, give money; to one for
whom it is fitting to put the food in that one's mouth, put it in.

Sifre on Parshat Re'eh

When you are asked in the world to come, 'What was your work?' and you
answer, 'I fed the hungry,' you will be told, 'This is the gate of the Lord, enter
into it, you who have fed the hungry.' Midrash Psalms 118:17

There is a Jewish joke that goes thus:

What's the story behind every Jewish holiday?
Someone tried to kill us, we survived, now let's eat!

Eating affirms life. *L'chaim! To life!* That's the drinking salute in
Judaism. But does our eating and drinking always affirm life? A
stands for Apple, but D stands for *Diazinon, Dicloran, Dicofol,*
Dimethoate, Diphenylamine (DPA) and *Disulfoton*, which are just
some of the pesticides found in that healthy apple (and that's only
the Ds). There is a beautiful Jewish tradition to cover the braided
bread at the Sabbath meal, so that it will not become embarrassed

when the blessing is made over the wine first. How much more embarrassing to fill that bread, and that meal, with pesticides that leach into our streams and destroy our natural world.

The Torah decree to separate between meat and milk, between the cooked flesh of the suckling and the milk from the mother's teat, trains us in sensitivity. Eating always involves taking, and taking requires responsibility. Though we may be able to masticate all types of food at one go, perhaps we ought to contemplate the source of the foods we eat, ask questions about decency and ethics before we tuck in.

Not only *what* we eat, but the *quantity* we eat is worth considering. The 11th century Jewish philosopher Maimonides advises that one should eat only:

> *Up to the point of feeling three quarters full.*
>
> The Book of Knowledge, Chapter 4.

Perhaps when we ourselves are overly satiated, we tend to forget the needs of the billions who are not.

Christian

'Give us this day our daily bread', is part of the Lord's Prayer Jesus taught his first disciples. The word 'bread' can be interpreted to mean all our needs, but bread is, of course, a basic requirement for many humans. It was part of the fundamental message Jesus gave in preparation for his departure.

That the Lord Jesus the same night in which he was betrayed took bread: And when he had given thanks, he brake it, and said, Take, eat: this is my body, which is broken for you: this do in remembrance of me. 1 Corinthians 11:23-24

Christians have used bread and wine to remember Jesus and his last supper as part of their basic worship ever since. These words are part of the Mass, Eucharist or Communion services:

We break this bread to share in the body of Christ. Though we are many, we are one body, because we all share in one bread.

In doing so Christians remember that both the bread and the wine used in the Eucharist are created from natural products of the earth, which are turned into bread and wine by human hands and so the Eucharist often includes these words:

Through your goodness we have this bread to offer which earth has given and human hands have made.

Humans can do amazing things with very basic ingredients. But a loss of a natural product or the introduction of an unnatural one through man's mismanagement could prove a disaster.

Unlike members of other faiths, Christians have few links with food in their worship and most are left to decide for example whether to be vegetarians for purely personal reasons. What few customs do exist are linked more to celebrations and events rather than for worship, such as Christmas cakes, simnel cakes and pascal cheesecakes. The custom of eating hot cross buns on Good Friday has now largely been forgotten as they are available throughout the year. One tradition, mainly associated with the Catholic Church, is eating fish rather than meat on Fridays. Many Christians will give up some form of food or drink during Lent.

Whilst food is fundamental to our well-being, if we are to love our neighbours we cannot enjoy our meals knowing that there are others whose plates are empty. The fact that we have sufficient is commemorated with prayers of gratitude before meals of which the simplest is:

For what we are about to receive may the Lord make us truly thankful.   Grace

Food is also an opportunity to show friendship, offer hospitality and enable families to be together; there is nothing uniquely Christian about that. Jesus chose a very special meal, where all his friends were gathered, to tell them that his end was nigh and taught them how to remember him. He chose no ordinary meal to become the Last Supper.

Muslim

The word for 'consume' in the Qur'an is the same as the word for 'eat'. You 'eat up' wealth as well as food. If we eat too much we consume more than food and it has more far-reaching effects than making us fat and unhealthy. It can result in other people being deprived of food. Much of what we eat in rich countries is imported from poorer ones where people often go hungry. If we eat too much meat, we encourage meat producers to feed to animals grain and other foods that other people could have eaten.

Muslims living in countries where there is little land to grow food may have to eat meat, especially sheep and goats, that feed on scrub and other plants no human can eat. Meat is a very important part of many Muslims' diet, but meat, like any other

food, should be eaten with restraint and moderation, and food should be shared out so that everyone has a little and no one gets too much. In countries where agricultural land is relatively plentiful, such as Egypt, everyday food normally consists of vegetables and fruit, and animals and birds are only killed and consumed on special occasions.

The Qur'an and the practice of the Prophet Muhammad (pbuh) teach Muslims that their food should be good and pure and animals for food should be killed in a quick and humane way so that they do not suffer. Intoxicating drinks and drugs are forbidden in the Qur'an and smoking is considered forbidden as harmful to the bodies God gave us. Muslims also fast to learn to restrain their appetites, but when some of the Prophet's Companions showed excessive zeal in fasting he told them, 'Your body has a right over you'.

Eat and drink, but do not be extravagant, for God does not love extravagant people.   Qur'an 7:31

Let man consider the food he eats! We pour down abundant water and cause the soil to split open. We make grain grow, and vines, fresh vegetation, olive trees, date palms, luscious gardens, fruits, and fodder: all for you and your livestock to enjoy.   Qur'an 80: 24-32

No man fills a pot worse than his stomach. For a person a few mouthfuls are sufficient to keep his back straight. But if he wants to fill his stomach then he should divide his stomach into three parts: He should fill one third of the belly with food, another third with drink and leave one third empty for easy breathing.   Hadith: Tirmidhi

The Prophet (pbuh) once said:

Whoever has food enough for two people, should take in a third one, and whoever has food enough for four persons, should take in a fifth or a sixth.

Hadith: Bukhari

The Caliph Umar said:

Beware of meat, because it has an addiction like the addiction of wine.

During his Caliphate, Umar prohibited people from eating meat two days in a row. He only allowed them to eat it every other day. One day he saw a man eating meat every day, and he said to him:

Every time you get hungry you go out and buy meat? he said, 'Yes, Amir al-Mumineen, I love meat.' And Umar said, 'It would be better for you to roll up your tummy a little bit so that other people can eat.' Hadith Malik: Muwatta Bab al-Laham, the Chapter of Meat

Examples, actions and ideas

❉ Grow your own – some of the very best vegetables and fruit are home grown. As well as having zero food miles, the whole process of preparing the ground, sowing the seeds and tending the young plants is a spiritual experience and one that brings friends, families and communities together. In London Capital Growth is an initiative to create food-growing spaces in the capital, (www.capitalgrowth.org).

Tomato flash grow
Trafalgar Square

❉ Keyhole gardens – developed to assist families in Africa (which may consist entirely of children) to produce food to live on, these are great for small spaces and can fit on balconies and doorsteps. The method of concentrating compost, manure and water in a small area works very well enabling produce to be easily fed and watered during a drought and raising crops above the general ground level which could be flooded during periods of heavy rain, (www.sendacow.org.uk/keyhole-gardens).

❋ Buy locally – farmers markets are good places to buy fresh produce grown locally, (www.localfoods.org.uk).

❋ Eat seasonally, remembering the air miles that are expended to bring summer fruits and vegetables out of season and energy required for refrigerated storage and heated greenhouses.

❋ Buy unpackaged food whenever possible, choosing fruit and veg off the shelf and taking your own bags to the market, your own cup to the coffee shop.

❋ Organically grown food which uses fewer, if any, chemicals and where most pesticides are banned offers the best, currently available, practical model for addressing climate-friendly food production.

❋ Choose sustainably sourced food – check where the fish, meat and fruit you buy come from.

❋ Eat less meat – UN figures suggest that meat production is responsible for about 18 per cent of global carbon emissions and health experts believe that reduced meat consumption would have positive effects on health through reductions in heart disease.

❋ The annual Jewish Food Conference in California, run by the environmental movement Hazon, is the only place in the world where farmers and rabbis, nutritionists and chefs, vegans and omnivores, come together to explore the dynamic interplay of food, Jewish tradition and contemporary life, (www.hazon.org).

Chapter 6

Biodiversity and Regeneration

The earth's biological diversity, its *biodiversity*, is vast beyond our imagination. As humans, we are the dominant element in that biodiversity alongside millions of other living species. Throughout the centuries we have been fascinated by the beauty and complexity of the earth's riches, seeking to understand them, but also recognising that despite all our knowledge and power, we are completely dependent on the creator of this fragile biological diversity. At last we are waking up to the realisation that our activities have already destroyed many species and more are at risk.

We still do not know the extent of the world's biodiversity in all its many forms involving untold species and subspecies. We do know that many have been lost and others face extinction for a variety of reasons. We also understand that the loss of one species can mean the loss of others which depend on it in some way. All life is interconnected and humankind is part of the network. Whilst we may feel superior to the rest of nature, it is only the power we have to despoil or protect that makes us so special.

We are all stewards and custodians of this precious and beautiful earth; it is a responsibility the scriptures have prepared us for well.

Jewish

Take up weeping and wailing for the mountains.
And a lamentation for the pastures of the wilderness,
Because they are laid waste so that no one passes through,
And the lowing of the cattle is not heard;
Both the birds of the air and the animals
Have fled and are gone.

Who is the man so wise that he can understand this? To whom has the mouth of the Lord spoken, that he may declare it? Why is the land ruined and laid waste like a wilderness, so that no one passes through? And the Lord says: Because they have forsaken my law which I set before them, and they have not obeyed my voice, or walked in accord with it, but have stubbornly followed their own hearts and have gone after the Baal – Idols, as their ancestors taught them.

Jeremiah 9:10 -14.

The words that the Prophet Jeremiah cried 2,500 years ago still ring true today. Every day another 50 animal species become extinct: the birds and animals have indeed fled and are gone. Every year another 400 plants species are lost: let us lament for the wild pastures gone forever.

There has been a catastrophic fall in rhino numbers.

When we idolise:

> *The work of our hands.*   Psalm 90

above our responsibility to the creator of all life, then we need no prophet to predict that sad future.

God created every plant, every animal, every soul with its own power and purpose, writes the great Jewish thinker, Nachmonides, in the 12th century. The sages of old tell us that every blade of grass has its own angel, which strikes it and says: 'Grow!' God cares about the details; we should too.

In the Torah, the need for biodiversity reached back to the first moment of human creation:

When God created man, God said 'Let us make man in our image, after our likeness.'   Genesis 1:26.

Traditionally, it is understood that God was speaking to the angels. If so, the plan was not very successful; we are not like angels. According to another interpretation, God was speaking to the whole of creation, to all of nature. In that case, 'Let us make man in our image' means, 'Let each of you contribute something.' The fox and the dove, the tiger and the sheep, the spider and the bee each contributed a small part—as did the angels and the devils. We humans contain all the parts.   Rabbi Adin Steinsaltz

By destroying even the smallest part of nature, we are deeply and truly destroying some component of our own humanity. However, comprising so many different pieces and parts, as we do, it can be hard to hold perspective. Saving tree frogs is important, but the loggers also need to feed their families. Dams destroy the salmon runs, but give farms the vital water they require. Religion does not spoon feed us the answer to these dilemmas, but it does offer us three value nodes towards a meaningful response.

The first is that the universe with each interlocking part is created for a *purpose*.

In all that God created in this world, the Holy One did not create a single thing without a purpose; thus the snail is a remedy for certain wounds, the fly can cure the hornet's sting, the mosquito (when crushed) alleviates a snake bite, the venom of the snake cures certain boils, and the spider's bite heals a scorpion's sting.

Babylonian Talmud, Shabbat 77b

The rabbinical sages compared creation to a garment of clothing, where the existence of each creature weaves so thoroughly into the warp and woof of the cloth itself, that removing a single thread alters the design entirely.

All that we see –
The heaven, the earth, and all that fills it –
All these things are the external garment of God.

Rebbe Shneur Zalman, Tanya 42

The second value is *humility*; a humble recognition that the purpose of this universe greatly exceeds our fathoming. The one who cuts down a Tasmanian Old Growth Eucalyptus tree for paper pulp may have made an informed choice, yet her hand should tremble in the choosing.

Why were human beings created last in the order of creation? So that they should not grow proud – for one can say to them, 'Even the gnat came before you in creation!'

Tosefta Sanhedrin 8:3

And third, the stewardship of a purpose driven universe is an *active* pursuit. 'Do no harm,' is not enough in a world that is not yet complete. Like Noah and family inside the ark, let's awaken like insomniacs to protect the last of each kind.

Avraham asked Shem (the son of Noah), 'How did you merit to survive in the ark (during the Biblical flood)?' 'Through charity,' Shem answered. 'But what kind of charity could you perform on an ark – there were certainly no poor people there?' replied Avraham. 'Charity to animals, beasts and birds!' answered Shem. 'We never slept, we tended each species at the proper time, all night long.'

Midrash Tehillim 37:1

Christian

Nature is a rich tapestry of species and sub-species all with their own uniqueness, purpose and heritage. Scientists say they are still far from identifying all the species within the forests of life, but we are often content to combine them into 'just a forest'. How can we even begin to count any loss when we have not yet managed to count or identify the current numbers?

There is much to be learned from the biodiversity of the species:

But ask now the beasts, and they shall teach thee; and the fowls of the air, and they shall tell thee: Or speak to the earth, and it shall teach thee: and the fishes of the sea shall declare unto thee. Who knoweth not in all these that the hand of the Lord hath wrought this? In whose hand is the soul of every living thing, and the breath of all mankind.   Job 12:7–10

Within the various Christian sects and traditions there is a variety of rules and regulations. With the translation of the Bible the biodiversity of our languages has also meant a wide range of interpretations of stories and parables. Words like 'stewardship' and 'dominion' are still being debated, as is just which is the seventh day. But 'nature' is the commonly accepted term for what most Christians would consider the basis for the goodness of the world – the provider of all its food, health and the quality of life.

You do not have to be of any faith to enjoy and appreciate nature. Most people will enjoy a garden, but it can be of little surprise to find a poet writing:

The kiss of the sun for pardon,
The song of the birds for mirth,
One is nearer God's heart in a garden
Than anywhere else on earth.　　　　　　Mrs Dorothy Frances Gurney

On Palm Sunday, the Sunday before Easter and the start of Holy Week, Christians distribute crosses made out of palm leaves as a reminder of how Jesus was welcomed by the crowds when he entered Jerusalem. Holly is the symbol of Christ's suffering, as, according to legend, it provided the wood for his cross.

Even the smallest green space can prove vital to us. That is why it is so important that Christian buildings which have land around them should make this available for peace and reflection. Then, however briefly, we can use this space to be able to link with nature. These 'green lungs' can provide the chance for a Sabbath moment – a time for rest and renewal in our lives.

The environment is God's gift to everyone, and in our use of it we have a responsibility towards the poor, towards future generations and towards humanity as a whole.   His Holiness, Pope Benedict XVI

Jesus began his life in a stable on a bed of straw. Whilst the gospels do not actually record it, the Christmas story includes the possibility that he shared the manger with animals. The gospels do record him being visited by shepherds and they may have brought their sheep with them to welcome Jesus, the Lamb of God – Agnus Dei.

Jesus knew the importance of nature and spent time alone in the desert for contemplation of the future. After the last supper he went to the Garden of Gethsemane where he was arrested and after his crucifixion he first appeared in a garden, at first being mistaken for a gardener – a second Adam.

If we begin from the belief that God wants us to rejoice and delight in the created world, our basic attitude to the environment will not be anxiety or the desperate search for ways of controlling it; it will be the excited and hopeful search for understanding it and honouring its goodness and its complex, interdependent beauty.   The Rt Revd Dr Rowan Williams

2000 year old olive trees in the Garden of Gethsemane

Muslim

Among His signs is the creation of the heavens and earth and all the living creatures He has scattered throughout them: He has the power to gather them all together whenever He wills.

Qur'an 42:29

All the creatures that crawl on the earth and those that fly with their wings are communities like yourselves.

Qur'an 6:38

Do they not look at the earth – how many noble things of all kinds We have produced therein?

Qur'an 26:7

When Our command came, and water gushed up out of the earth, We said, 'Place on board this Ark a pair of each species, and your own family.'

Qur'an 11:40

The Prophet (pbuh) said:

An ant bit one of the prophets, and he ordered that the place of the ants be burnt. So, Allah inspired to him, 'Is it because one ant bit you that you would burn one of the nations that glorify Allah?'

Hadith: Bukhari

Umar Ibn al-Khattab heard the Prophet Muhammad (pbuh) say:

Allah who is great and glorious created a thousand species, six hundred in the sea and four hundred on the land. The first species to perish will be the locusts, and when they perish the species will follow one another like beads on a string.

Hadith: Bayhaqi

God has given us all the wonderful and diverse species of animals that inhabit the earth. The Qur'an tells us that:

Everything in the heavens and earth bows down to God: the sun, the moon, the stars, the mountains, the trees, and the animals? So do many human beings.

Qur'an 22:18

He has made His creatures tame for us so that we can use them. If He wished, He could change all this, making them hostile to human beings or taking them away. A Millennium Assessment Board statement of March 2005, (the work of more than 1,360 experts worldwide, called for by the United Nations) called 'Living Beyond Our Means' states that:

Human activities have taken the planet to the edge of a massive wave of species extinctions, further threatening our own well-being.

We human beings are living so carelessly that we pollute and destroy habitats like oceans, forests and wetlands. Starving bears, seagulls, Komodo dragons and other creatures are moving further into human habitations to survive as their natural food supplies

are destroyed. Turtles and albatrosses are choking and starving through eating waste plastic in the sea. God's creatures are dying in huge numbers. We humans have no power to restore them to life.

In the next world we will have to account for our ill-treatment of God's creatures; The Prophet Muhammad (pbuh) said:

If anyone kills a sparrow or anything greater wrongfully, Allah will question him about killing it.   Hadith: Ahmad, Nasa'i and Darimi

Corruption has appeared on land and sea as a result of people's actions and He will make them taste the consequences of some of their own actions so that they may turn back.   Qur'an 30:41

The Prophet Muhammad (pbuh) said:

A woman was punished and put into Hell because of a cat which she had kept locked in until it died of hunger.   Hadith: Bukhari

Unless we all respect and behave with more care for the earth and all the communities of plants, animals and people that God created in a just balance (Qur'an 55:7), we, like Noah's people, may well find our own habitats threatened in this world as well as the next.

Albatross in flight

Examples, actions, ideas

- Plan for biodiversity – leave existing wildlife habitats intact when making changes and introduce elements such as ponds, marshes, safe corridors for animals, amphibians and reptiles to get around.
- Plant for biodiversity – even the smallest green space can have a real effect on the birds, bees and other insects and some plants are particularly necessary to the survival of some species.
- Green and brown roofs provide an important refuge for wildlife in the UK urban environment and can be planned for when creating new buildings and considered for existing ones.
- Native trees and shrubs help support the indigenous insect and bird life.
- H*ima* reserves are traditional areas in Saudi Arabia which have been managed sustainably since early Islamic times and are among the most long-standing examples of rangeland and woodland conservation known.

Yews at St Edward's Paris
Church, Stow on the Wol

Glossary

Abraham
Jews regard Abraham as the first Patriarch of the Jewish people.
He was the first person to teach the idea that there was only one
God.

Abrahamic faiths
The world's three primary monotheistic faiths – Judaism,
Christianity and Islam.

Adam
The first man created by God in the Abrahamic faiths.

Adaptation Fund
The Adaptation Fund was established to finance concrete
adaptation projects and programmes in developing countries that
are Parties to the Kyoto Protocol.

Aishah
Aishah bint Abi Bakr was the youngest wife of Muhammad.

Akhirah
The next life (Islam).

Allah
The name Muslims use for the supreme and unique God, who
created and sustains everything.

Amanah
Trust (Islam).

Anglican Creed
Creeds are statements of Christians' basic beliefs about God. The Anglican Church uses two creeds in its worship: The Apostles' Creed and the Nicene Creed.

Apostolic Nuncio
The ambassador of the Holy See to a state or organisation, usually with the ecclesiastical rank of archbishop.

Ash Wednesday
The first day of Lent in the Christian calendar. The name is derived from the practice of marking an ash cross on the forehead as a mark of repentance.

Aspergill
Brush or branch used in Christian blessing to scatter Holy Water.

Avot
A compilation of the ethical teachings of the Rabbis of the Mishnaic period.

Avraham
Abraham.

Ba'al Shem Tov
A Jewish mystical rabbi of the 17th and 18th centuries.

Bal Taschit
The Torah's prohibition on wasteful or pointless destruction of property or resources.

Baal-idols
Idols used in the worship of Baal, a Phoenician deity.

Bible
The Bible is the book containing the Hebrew or Christian sacred scriptures which are central to the Jewish and Christian faiths. The Christian Bible consists of the Old and New Testaments.

Book of Common Prayer
The title of a number of prayer books used by most churches in the Anglican Communion.

Caliph Umar ibn al-Khattab
The second successor to the Prophet Muhammad (pbuh) and one of the 'rightly guided' Muslim rulers.

Canticle
A hymn from the Bible.

Chief Rabbi
The leader of the Jewish community in Britain.

Christian liturgy
The pattern for Christian worship.

Church of England
The established Church in England and the Mother Church for the Anglican Communion.

Covenant
Agreement between God and his people.

Crucifixion
The execution of Jesus Christ on the cross.

Daniel, Book of
Relates the visions and narratives of the prophet Daniel who lived during the Babylonian captivity, which began in 597 BC.

David Ben Gurion
Israel's first prime minister.

Desert of Midian
Thought to be in northwest Arabia to which Moses fled to escape
the Pharoah.

Deuteronomy, Book of
The fifth of the Five Books of Moses (see Torah), which contains
the code of law by which the Israelites were to live in the
Promised Land.

Dunya
This life (Islam).

Ecclesiastical Year
The cycle of seasons celebrated by the Church during the year.

Ecumenical Patriarch
First amongst equals, the highest see and holiest centre of the
Orthodox Christian Church throughout the world.

Eden
Name given by Jews and Christians to the 'earthly paradise'
occupied by Adam and Eve before their fall through sin. To
Muslims, Eden is not the name of an earthly garden but an
adjective meaning 'lasting', applying to the rewards good people
will receive in the next world.

Encyclical
Circular letter sent to all churches. In the Roman Catholic church
it relates to a letter sent by the Pope, usually relating to some
aspect of Catholic doctrine.

Eucharist
Christian communion service.

Exodus, Book of
The second book of the Torah and Christian Bible relating the exodus of the Israelites from Egypt.

Font
A baptismal font in a church containing holy water. In some churches the font is large enough for total immersion.

Flood, The
In the Old Testament, Hebrew Bible and Qu'ran a deluge lasting 40 days and 40 nights which obliterated everyone and everything apart from those in Noah's Ark.

Garden of Gethsemane
The garden at the foot of the Mount of Olives in Jerusalem where Jesus and his disciples prayed the night before his crucifixion.

Genesis, Book of
The first book of the Hebrew Bible and Old Testament in which many of the best known stories including the creation and Noah's Ark appear.

Good Friday
The Friday before Easter commemorating the crucifixion of Jesus.

Gospels
Generally describing the first four books of the New Testament telling the story of the life of Jesus and written by his disciples Matthew, Mark, Luke and John.

Hadith
The Hadith are reports of the sayings and deeds of Prophet Muhammad and his companions and are an important source for religious practice, law, and traditions.

Hildegard of Bingen
Venerated nun and polymath, Hildegard was an artist, scholar and composer who died in 1179.

Holy Communion
The Eucharist, the Christian sacrament celebrated as a re-enactment of Jesus's Last Supper of bread and wine.

Holy See
The diocese of the Pope. The Roman Catholic Bishopric of Rome.

Holy Water
Water blessed for religious uses.

Honi
Early Jewish scholar.

Ibrahim
The Arabic name for the prophet Abraham.

IHS
Christian symbol representing the name of Jesus in Greek.

Islam
The world's second largest religion with over 1 billion followers.

Isma'il
The son of Ibrahim.

Jeremiah
Prophet from Old Testament and Hebrew Bible. His writings are contained in the Book of Jeremiah.

Jesus Christ
Christians believe Jesus was the son of God and the Messiah who was foretold in the Old Testament.

John the Baptist
St John the Baptist preached on the banks of the Jordan against the evils of the times and called men to baptism. He recognised Jesus as the Messiah and baptised him.

Ka'ba
The first house of worship built by Ibrahim and Ismail for the One God, a cuboid building at the centre of the quadrangle of the Great Mosque in Mecca.

Khutbah
Sermon (Islam).

King James Bible
The original translation of the Bible was published in 1611 in the reign of James VI and I and the 'Authorised edition' in 1769.

Kyoto Protocol
The Kyoto Protocol is an international agreement linked to the United Nations Framework Convention on Climate Change. It was adopted in Kyoto, Japan, on 11 December 1997 and entered into force on 16 February 2005.

Lamb, The
John the Baptist described Jesus as 'the Lamb of God that takes away the sins of the world' (John 1:29), referring to his sacrifice; Agnus Dei in Latin.

Last Supper
The last meal Jesus shared with his disciples before his death.

Lauds
Morning worship in the Christian liturgy.

Lent
The period of 40 days, excluding Sundays, which comes before Easter in the Christian calendar.

Leviticus, Book of
The third book in the Hebrew Bible and Old Testament which contains laws and priestly rituals.

Liturgical Calendar
Determines when feast days and saints' days are observed and which portions of Scripture are to be read.

Lord's Prayer, The
The prayer taught by Jesus to his disciples.

Maimonides
Medieval Jewish philosopher and Torah scholar.

Mass
The celebration of the Christian Eucharist.

Matthew, Book of
The first book of the New Testament, one of the four Gospels.

Mecca
The city in Arabia where Muslims believe Ibrahim and Ishmael built the first house of worship for the One God. Muslims face it in all their prayers and must make a pilgrimage to it at least once in their lifetime if they can.

Midrash
Biblical allegory.

Mizan
Balance of creation and justice.

Monotheism
Belief or doctrine that there is only one God.

Moses
One of Judaism's great figures, the channel between God and the Hebrews, through whom the Hebrews received a basic charter for living as God's people. Moses is mentioned in the Qur'an as a messenger of God.

Muslim Declaration
Created in Assisi in 1986 when five leaders of the five major world religions on Nature – Buddhism, Christianity, Hinduism, Islam and Judaism – met to discuss how their faiths could help save the natural world.

Nachmonides
Great Spanish Torah scholar who lived from 1194-1270.

New Testament
The second part of the Christian Bible, the New Testament has 27 books and records the life and teachings of Christ and his followers.

Noah
Figure from the Old Testament and Hebrew Bible and the Qur'an who built an ark, or ship, according to God's instructions so his family and specimens of all living creatures could survive the Flood. Noah is mentioned in the Qur'an as a messenger of God.

Office
Act of worship; the order or form of religious service.

Old Testament
The first section of the Christian Bible, the Old Testament is the original Hebrew Bible, the sacred scriptures of the Jewish faith.

Orthodox Church
One of the three main Christian groups (the others being Roman Catholic and Protestant).

Palm Sunday
At the beginning of Holy Week, leading up to Easter, Palm Sunday commemorates Jesus's triumphant arrival in Jerusalem where the crowd waved palm branches in greeting.

Parable
A fable or story told to illustrate a moral or religious point.

PBUH
Muslims often use the phrase, 'Peace be upon him' (pbuh) after saying the name of a prophet of Islam as a sign of respect eg, 'Prophet Muhammad (pbuh).'

Prophet Muhammad
Muslims believe the final and complete revelation of the Islam faith was made through the Prophet Muhammad who was born in Mecca in Arabia in 570.

Prophet, The
In Islam, Muhammad (pbuh) is believed to be the last and greatest of a long line of prophets which began with Adam and included Jesus.

Psalms
Sacred poems. The Book of Psalms in the Old Testament and Hebrew Bible contains 150 psalms.

Qanat
Underground tunnel for carrying irrigation water.

Qur'an
The holy book for Muslims which was revealed over 23 years to the Prophet Muhammad (pbuh).

Rabbi
A Jewish religious leader.

Rabbi Adin Steinsaltz
Noted rabbi, scholar and philosopher born in 1937.

Rabbi Nachman of Bratslav
Famous Jewish leader who lived from 1772 to 1810.

Rabbi Samson Raphael Hirsch
Renowned German Jewish leader of the nineteenth century.

Rashi
Rabbi Solomon Yitzchaki, the great Biblical and Talmudic commentator, who was born in France in 1040.

Rebbe Schneur Zalman of Liadi
Founder of Chabad, a branch of Hasidic Judaism, and a prolific author.

Revelation, Book of
The last book of the New Testament which contains vivid imagery of disaster and suffering and the conflict between good and evil.

Richard the Lionheart
Richard 1 King of England from 1189, also known as the Lionheart for his bravery in the Third Crusade.

Roman Catholic Church
The world's largest Christian church with more than a billion members. Its leader in matters of faith, morality, and governance is the Pope.

Saladin
Great Muslim leader who recaptured Jerusalem for the Muslims in 1187.

Shabbat
Starting at sunset on Friday evening and ending on Saturday at nightfall, the Shabbat or Sabbath is the day Jews remember the seventh day of creation on which God rested.

Shari'ah
Islamic law.

Simnel cake
A light fruit cake covered in marzipan made for Mothering Sunday.

Sodom and Gomorrah
Ancient cities in the Middle East destroyed by fire and brimstone for their wickedness according to Genesis.

Stoup
Vessel for Holy Water.

Talmud
The summary of Jewish oral law and lore that evolved over centuries of scholarly effort by the sages who lived in Palestine and Babylonia until the beginning of the Middle Ages.

Tawhid
The concept of monotheism and the doctrine of God's Oneness in Islam.

Ten Commandments
Laws given by God to Moses on Mount Sinai.

Third Pillar of Islam
Zakat, or almsgiving. A religious obligation.

Torah
The first five books of the Hebrew Bible, ascribed to Moses. The Torah is also known by its Greek appellation: the Pentateuch. These five books are: Genesis, Exodus, Leviticus, Numbers, and Deuteronomy. The scrolls on which the Torah is hand written are housed in an ark, a sacred enclosure, in every synagogue.

Tree of Life
A*rbor vitae*, a tree in the Garden of Eden whose fruit gave everlasting life (Genesis 2:9).

Ummah
The Muslim community.

Vayikra Rabbah
A collection of stories inspired by the narrative of the Book of Vayikra (Hebrew for Leviticus).

Zakat
Obligatory wealth tax to be paid by all who can afford it to help the poor and needy, travellers, new converts to Islam, etc. The word implies purification.

Useful Contacts

Jewish

* **The Big Green Jewish Website** is a resource for Jewish people, which campaigns to raise awareness about environmental issues in the Jewish community, (www.biggreenjewish.org).

* **Jewish Climate Change Campaign** is a call to action, a call to demonstrate that the Jewish people can help light the way to more sustainable living, (www.jewishclimatecampaign.org).

* **The Jew and the Carrot** is an online resource tackling the relationship between Judaism, food and climate change, (www.jcarrot.org).

Christian

* **A Rocha** is a Christian environmental and nature conservation movement, (www.arocha.org).

* **Eco-Congregation** is an ecumenical programme helping churches make the link between environmental issues and Christian faith, and respond in practical action in the church, in the lives of individuals, and in the local and global community, (www.ecocongregation.org).

* **European Christian Environmental Network** (ECEN) is a church network promoting co-operation in caring for creation, (www.ecen.org).

❊ **Operation Noah** is a Christian organisation which provides focus and leadership in response to the threat of climate change, (www.operationnoah.org).

❊ **The Interfaith Power and Light** campaign, part of the Regeneration Project in the United States, is mobilising a religious response to global warming in congregations through the promotion of renewable energy, energy efficiency, and conservation, (www.interfaithpowerandlight.org).

❊ **The John Ray Initiative** is an educational charity connecting Environment, Science and Christianity, (www.jri.org.uk).

❊ **Shrinking the Footprint** is the Church of England's national environmental campaign, (www.shrinkingthefootprint.org).

Muslim

❊ **The Islamic Foundation for Ecology and Environmental Sciences** (IFEES) is dedicated to the maintenance of the earth as a healthy habitat for all living things, (www.ifees.org.uk).

❊ **Wisdom in Nature** is an ecological and community activism group guided by Islamic principles, (www.wisdominnature.org.uk).

❊ **Midlands Islamic Network for the Environment** aims to increase environmental awareness, share information and provide training and social events, (www.muslimbirmingham. wordpress.com/mine-and-homeplanet-show).

❊ **Reading Islamic Trustees for the Environment** is a community group whose vision is to bring a wider appreciation of our environment, (www.rite.btck.co.uk).

❖ **EcoMuslim** wants to change behaviours on an individual, organisational, societal, national, regional and global levels to preserve the Earth's ecosystems, natural resources, beauty and environment, (www.ecomuslim.com).

Multifaith

❖ **ARC**, the Alliance of Religions and Conservation is a secular body that helps religions link with key environmental organisations creating powerful alliances between faith communities and conservation groups, (www.arcworld.org).

❖ **CIWEM**'s (The Chartered Institution of Water and Environmental Management) Faiths and the Environment network was set up in 2009 to put belief systems at the heart of environmental policy and action, (www.ciwem.org).

❖ **Faith Climate Connect** is a free global resource and network, bringing together an interactive forum of videos, faith and climate news, scriptural references, video conferencing, instant messaging, photographs and blogs. It is the brainchild of the Bible Society in association with Odyssey Networks, the New York based non-profit coalition of Christian, Jewish and Muslim faith groups, (www.faithclimateconnect.com).

Publications

❖ How Many Lightbulbs Does It Take to Change a Christian?
  and Don't Stop At The Lights, both by Claire Foster and
  David Shreeve, published by Church House Publishing,
  (www.chpublishing.co.uk).

❖ The Muslim Green Guide to Reducing Climate Change
  (www.ifees.org.uk) and follow links via Resources tab.

❖ Jesus and the Earth by James Jones, Bishop of Liverpool,
  published by SPCK, (www.spck.org.uk).

❖ Teachers' Guide Book for Islamic Environmental Education by Fazlun
  Khalid and Ali Kh Thani, published by The Islamic Foundation
  for Ecology & Environmental Sciences, (www.ifees.org.uk).

❖ What Will You Do? 48 Things You Can Do To Make A Difference.
  Published by the Jewish Responsibility Project at the London
  School of Jewish Studies, (www.lsjs.ac.uk).

❖ A Jewish Guide to Fairtrade, compiled by Poppy Berelowitz.
  Published by Fairtrade Foundation, (www.fairtrade.org.uk).

❖ Sharing God's Planet, a Christian vision for a sustainable
  future. Published by Church House Publishing,
  (www.chpublishing.co.uk).

❖ 199 Ways to Please God by Rianne ten Veen, is a Muslim guide to
  sustainability and is available from www.amazon.co.uk.

Photographs